fast simple
family
meals

TRIDENT PRESS
INTERNATIONAL

Published by:
TRIDENT PRESS INTERNATIONAL
801, 12th Avenue South
Suite 302
Naples, FL 34102 U.S.A.
Copyright (c)Trident Press International 2001
Tel: (941) 649 7077
Fax: (941) 649 5832
Email: tridentpress@worldnet.att.net
Website: www.trident-international.com

acknowledgements

Fast Simple Family Meals

Compiled by: R&R Publications Marketing Pty. Ltd.
Creative Director: Paul Sims
Production Manager: Anthony Carroll
Food Photography: Warren Webb, William Meppem,
Andrew Elton, Quentin Bacon,
Gary Smith, Per Ericson, Paul Grater, Ray Joice,
John Stewart, Ashley Mackevicius, Harm Mol,
Yanto Noerianto, Andy Payne.
Food Stylists: Stephane Souvlis, Janet Lodge, Di Kirby,
Wendy Berecry, Belinda Clayton, Rosemary De Santis,
Carolyn Fienberg, Jacqui Hing, Michelle Gorry,
Christine Sheppard, Donna Hay.
Recipe Development: Ellen Argyriou, Sheryle Eastwood,
Kim Freeman, Lucy Kelly, Donna Hay, Anneka Mitchell,
Penelope Peel, Jody Vassallo, Belinda Warn, Loukie Werle.
Proof Reader: Andrea Tarttelin

Includes Index
ISBN 1582791619
EAN 9781582791616

First Edition Printed June 2001
Computer Typeset in Humanist 521 & Times New Roman

Printed in Hong Kong

Contents

introduction

Fast simple *family meals*

There's a great deal of nostalgia for honest-to-goodness family cooking: hearty soups, pastas and satisfying family favourites, complete with desserts and an array of fresh vegetables.

Everyday Family Meals includes all the old favourites, but because we live in an era where the cooking is likely to be shared by the whole family, and time is often a commodity more sought after than rare spices, the book also contains plenty of ideas for speedy snacks, salads both simple and sumptuous, and recipes for pasta and pizzas that can be made at home in less time than it takes to telephone for a takeaway.

We all aim to eat less meat and more fresh fruit and vegetables, but it isn't always easy to persuade the family to eat up their greens. The first step to a solution is provided by the chapter on salads and sides, where convenience foods are combined with fresh produce to provide a mouthwatering selection of side dishes.

Photograph page 5 also appears on recipe page 24 (Spaghetti with tuna and olives)

prawn (shrimp) bisque

soups
&
snacks

The door bangs, bags are dropped

in the hall, and the cry goes up: "What is there to eat?
Where starving!" Stave off post-school starvation with
this selection of soups and snacks.

leek
and mushroom soup

ingredients

45g/1¹/₂oz butter
2 leeks, thinly sliced
1 tablespoon yellow mustard seeds
250g/8oz button mushrooms, sliced
2 tablespoons chopped fresh thyme or
2 teaspoons dried thyme
4 cups/1 litre/1³/₄pt vegetable stock
125g/4oz risoni pasta
¹/₂ cup/125mL/4fl oz cream (double)

Method:

1 Melt butter in a large saucepan over a medium heat, add leeks and mustard seeds and cook, stirring, for 5 minutes or until leeks are soft and golden.
2 Add mushrooms and thyme to pan and cook for 5 minutes longer. Add stock and pasta, bring to the boil, then reduce heat and simmer for 15 minutes or until pasta is tender. Stir in cream and simmer for 5 minutes longer.

Serves 4

prawn
(shrimp) bisque

Photograph page 7

ingredients

315g/10oz cooked prawns (shrimp), shelled and deveined
¹/₂ onion, diced
¹/₂ cup/125mL/4fl oz tomato paste (purée)
2¹/₂ cups/600mL/1pt chicken stock
¹/₃ cup/90mL/3fl oz cream (double)
¹/₄ teaspoon paprika
freshly ground black pepper
1-2 tablespoons dry sherry

Method:

1 Place prawns (shrimp), onion and tomato paste (purée) in a food processor or blender and process to make a purée. With machine running, slowly add stock and process to combine.
2 Place prawn (shrimp) mixture in a saucepan and cook over a low heat, stirring frequently, for 10 minutes or until the mixture comes to the boil.
3 Stir in cream, paprika and black pepper to taste and cook for 2 minutes or until heated through. Stir in sherry and serve immediately.

Serves 6

mexican
corn chowder

Method:

1 Melt butter in a large saucepan and cook bacon, onion, celery and chilli for 4-5 minutes or until onion softens.
2 Add stock, cumin and thyme, bring to the boil and simmer for 10 minutes.
3 Stir in flour mixture, then milk and corn kernels, stir continuously until boiling, then reduce heat and simmer for 3 minutes. Season to taste with pepper.

ingredients

10g/¹/₃oz butter
2 rashers bacon,
rind removed and chopped
1 onion, finely chopped
2 stalks celery, chopped
1 small red chilli, finely chopped
2 cups/500mL chicken stock
1 teaspoon ground cumin
1 teaspoon dried thyme
2 tablespoons flour blended with
3 tablespoons milk
1³/₄ cups/440mL milk
440g/14oz canned sweet corn kernels,
drained
freshly ground black pepper

hot ham
sandwiches

Photograph page 11

ingredients

**2 x 10cm/4in squares focaccia bread or
2 small French bread sticks
185g/6oz ricotta cheese, drained
250g/8oz smoked ham, sliced
60g/2oz sun-dried tomatoes, sliced
3 tablespoons chopped fresh basil
30g/1oz fresh Parmesan cheese
shavings**

Method:

1 *Split focaccia bread or French bread sticks horizontally and spread each half with ricotta cheese. Top with ham, sun-dried tomatoes, basil and Parmesan cheese shavings. Place under a preheated hot grill and cook for 3-4 minutes or until cheese melts and is golden.*

Serving suggestion: *Serve with a fresh mushroom salad. To make mushroom salad, place sliced button mushrooms and chopped red pepper in a bowl. Toss with lemon juice, olive oil, chopped fresh parsley or chives, minced garlic and a pinch of chilli powder. Set aside to marinate while preparing and cooking the sandwiches.*

Note: *Cottage cheese can be used in place of ricotta cheese if you wish and fresh tomatoes or sliced black olives are good alternatives to the sun-dried tomatoes. To make Parmesan cheese shavings.*

Serves 4

grilled
banana sandwiches

Photograph page 11

ingredients

**8 slices rye or Granary bread
2 bananas, sliced
1 avocado, sliced
8 slices Gruyère cheese**

Method:

1 *Place bread under a preheated hot grill and cook for 2-3 minutes or until toasted on one side. Top untoasted side with bananas, avocado and cheese. Place under grill and cook for 3-4 minutes longer or until cheese melts and is golden.*

Serving suggestion: *Serve with a cos lettuce and bacon salad. To make salad, grill 1-2 rashers bacon and break into pieces. Separate leaves of 1 cos lettuce, tear into large pieces and place in a salad bowl. Sprinkle with bacon pieces, 2-3 tablespoons croûtons and 2-3 tablespoons grated Parmesan cheese. Drizzle salad with a creamy dressing.*

Serves 4

hot chicken
sandwiches

Photograph below

Method:

1 *Spread toast with mayonnaise and top with chicken, asparagus, black pepper to taste and cheese. Place under a preheated hot grill and cook for 3-4 minutes or until cheese melts and is golden.*

Serving suggestion: *Accompany with a bowl of canned soup and a salad of mixed lettuces and chopped fresh herbs tossed with a French dressing.*

Note: *Dress up canned soup by sprinkling with croûtons or fresh herbs. Prepared croûtons are available from supermarkets and are a useful ingredient to keep in your pantry for garnishing soups and salads.*

Serves 4

ingredients

8 slices wholemeal or white bread, toasted
4 tablespoons mayonnaise
500g/1 lb cooked chicken, skin removed and flesh shredded
440g/14oz canned asparagus spears, drained
freshly ground black pepper
8 slices Swiss cheese, such as Emmental or Gruyère

crusty
chicken salad rolls

Photograph page 13

Method:

1 *To make salad, place mayonnaise, dressing and mustard in a bowl and mix to combine. Add chicken, apples, eggs, celery, spring onions and parsley. Season to taste with black pepper and toss to combine.*

2 *Cut rolls in half and spread bases with mayonnaise. Top with salad, then place other halves on top.*

   Note: *For a tropical chicken salad, add 125g/4oz canned diced mangoes or peaches. In summer fresh peaches or mangoes are also delicious additions.*

   Serves 4

ingredients

4 large crusty bread rolls
4 tablespoons mayonnaise

Chicken salad
¹/₂ cup/125mL/4fl oz mayonnaise
2 tablespoons vinaigrette dressing
1 teaspoon French mustard
1 cooked chicken, skinned, boned and cut into small pieces
2 eating apples, peeled, cored and diced
2 hard-boiled eggs, diced
2 stalks celery, sliced thinly
2 spring onions, shredded
1 tablespoon chopped fresh parsley
freshly ground black pepper

smoked
salmon crossiants

Photograph page 13

Method:

1 *To make filling, place cream cheese and sour cream into a bowl and beat until smooth. Add salmon, spring onion, dill, capers and lime or lemon juice and mix to combine.*

2 *Top bottom half of each croissant with filling, then place other halves on top.*

   Serves 4

ingredients

4 croissants, split

Smoked salmon filling
155g/5oz cream cheese, softened
¹/₄ cup/60g/2oz sour cream
155g/5oz sliced smoked salmon, chopped
1 spring onion, thinly sliced
3 teaspoons chopped fresh dill
2 teaspoons capers, drained and chopped
2 teaspoons lime or lemon juice

cheesy noodles

fasta pasta

Simple and speedy to prepare,

*inexpensive, satisfying and extremely versatile –
there can be few ingredients with so much to offer
as pasta. As the recipes in this chapter prove,
pasta is equally happy when topped with a simple
sauce or as the basis for a hearty family bake.*

spaghetti
with pesto

Method:

1 Combine basil, pine nuts, garlic, sugar and salt in a blender or food processor. Process briefly to mix. With motor running, gradually add oil through lid or feeder tube, as when making mayonnaise. The mixture will form a thick sauce. Scrape pesto into a bowl or jug, cover and set aside.
2 Bring a large saucepan of lightly salted water to the boil. Add spaghetti and cook until just tender.
3 Drain spaghetti and tip it into a heated bowl. Add pesto and toss until all the spaghetti is evenly coated. Serve at once, garnished with fresh basil.

Serves 6

ingredients

**60g/2oz fresh basil leaves, plus basil sprigs for garnish
3 tablespoons pine nuts
4 cloves garlic, crushed
$^1/_4$ teaspoon sugar
$^1/_2$ teaspoon salt
5 tablespoon mild olive oil
375g/12oz spaghetti**

cheesy
noodles

Photograph page 15

ingredients

**2 x 90g/3oz packets quick-cooking noodles
4 tablespoons sour cream
freshly ground black pepper
60g/2oz tasty cheese
(mature cheddar), grated**

Method:

1 Prepare noodles according to packet directions. Drain, add sour cream and black pepper to taste and toss to combine.
2 Divide noodle mixture between two heatproof serving dishes and sprinkle with cheese. Place under a preheated hot grill and cook for 3-4 minutes until cheese melts and is golden.

Serving suggestion: Accompany with a salad made of the lettuce or lettuces of your choice, cherry tomatoes, chopped or sliced red or green peppers and chopped or sliced cucumber tossed with a French dressing.

Note: Mixtures of fresh salad greens are available from many greengrocers and supermarkets. These are an economical and easy alternative to buying a variety of lettuces and making your own salads of mixed lettuce leaves.

Serves 2

curried
vegetable salad

Method:
1 Cook pasta in boiling water in a large saucepan following packet directions. Drain, rinse under cold running water and cool completely.
2 Boil, steam or microwave broccoli and carrots separately until just tender. Drain and refresh under cold running water. Drain again and place in a serving bowl. Add zucchini (courgettes), red pepper, spring onions and pasta and toss to combine.
3 To make dressing, place mayonnaise, mustard, lemon juice, curry powder and black pepper to taste in a bowl and mix to combine. Spoon dressing over salad and toss to combine. Serve at room temperature.
Note: This dish makes a great vegetarian main meal when served with a tossed green salad and crusty bread or serve it as an accompaniment to grilled chicken or meat.

ingredients

250g/8oz macaroni
250g/8oz broccoli,
cut into small florets
2 carrots, cut into matchsticks
2 zucchini (courgettes),
cut into matchsticks
1 red pepper, cut into thin strips
2 spring onions, thinly sliced

Curry dressing
4 tablespoons mayonnaise
1 tablespoon French mustard
1 tablespoon lemon juice
1/2 teaspoon curry powder
freshly ground black pepper

creamy
pea and ham pasta
Photograph page 19

Method:

1 *Cook pasta in boiling water in a large saucepan following packet directions. Drain, set aside and keep warm.*

2 *Boil, steam or microwave peas until just cooked.*

3 *Place pasta, peas, ham and cream in a frying pan and heat over a medium heat, stirring frquently, for 5 minutes or until heated through. Season to taste with black pepper. Sprinkle with Parmesan cheese and serve immediately.*

Note: *Fresh Parmesan cheese is available from Continental delicatessens and some supermarkets. It is best purchased in a piece, then grated as required. Fresh Parmesan cheese has a milder and better flavour than the grated powder that comes in packets.*

Serves 4

ingredients

500g/1 lb linguine, spaghetti or other thin pasta of your choice
155g/5oz shelled fresh or frozen peas
250g/8oz diced ham
1 cup/250mL/8fl oz cream (double)
freshly ground black pepper
grated fresh Parmesan cheese

speedy
lasagne
Photograph page 19

Method:

1 *Heat oil in frying pan over a medium heat, add beef and cook, stirring constantly, to break up, for 5 minutes or until beef is brown. Drain off excess fat and stir in pasta sauce. Bring to simmering and simmer, stirring occasionally, for 10 minutes.*

2 *Place ricotta cheese, parsley, egg and black pepper to taste in a bowl and mix well to combine.*

3 *Spread one-third of the meat sauce over base of a lightly greased ovenproof dish, top with one-third lasagne sheets, cutting to fit as necessary, and one-third ricotta cheese mixture, then sprinkle with one-third mozzarella cheese and one-third Parmesan cheese. Repeat layers, to use all ingredients, finishing with a layer of cheese. Bake for 25 minutes or until top is golden and lasagne is hot.*

Note: *If fresh lasagne is unavailable instant (no precooking required) lasagne can be used instead. When using this type of lasagne dip the lasagne sheets in warm water before assembling.*

For a complete meal serve with garlic bread and a fresh green salad.

Serves 6

ingredients

2 tablespoons olive oil
250g/8oz lean ground beef
3 cups/750mL/1 1/4pt bottled tomato pasta sauce
500g/1 lb ricotta cheese, drained
2 tablespoons chopped fresh parsley
1 egg
freshly ground black pepper
500g/1 lb fresh lasagne sheets
500g/1 lb grated mozzarella cheese
125g/4oz grated Parmesan cheese

Oven temperature 180°C, 350°F, Gas 4

cheesy
pasta bake

Method:

1 Place hot pasta and 125g/4oz cheese in a lightly greased ovenproof dish, mix to combine and set aside.

2 Cook ham in a nonstick frying pan for 3-4 minutes. Add mushrooms and cook for 3 minutes longer. Spoon ham mixture over pasta and top with pasta sauce and basil. Combine breadcrumbs and remaining cheese. Sprinkle cheese mixture over pasta and bake for 20 minutes.

Serving suggestion: Accompany with a broccoli and cauliflower salad. To make salad, combine 2 tablespoons lemon juice, 2 teaspoons Dijon mustard, 3 tablespoons olive oil, 1 tablespoon finely chopped fresh parsley and black pepper to taste and toss with cooked broccoli and cauliflower florets.

Note: For quicker preparation, buy products that are partly prepared - cubed meat, grated cheese, instant (no precooking required) lasagne and boned chicken. Many supermarkets and greengrocers also sell fresh salads and vegetable mixes for soups and casseroles.

Serves 4

ingredients

**500g/1 lb pasta of your choice, cooked
220g/7oz tasty cheese
(mature cheddar), grated
8 slices ham, shredded
250g/8oz button mushrooms, sliced
750g/1½ lb jar tomato pasta sauce
2 tablespoons chopped fresh basil
30g/1oz breadcrumbs,
made from stale bread**

Oven temperature 200°C, 400°F, Gas 6

pasta
puttanesca

Method:

1 Cook pasta in boiling water in a large saucepan following packet directions. Drain, set aside and keep warm.

2 To make sauce, heat oil in a saucepan over a low heat, add garlic and cook, stirring, for 2 minutes. Add tomatoes and bring to the boil, then stir in anchovies, black olives, capers, oregano and chilli powder and simmer for 3 minutes longer. Spoon sauce over hot pasta, sprinkle with parsley and Parmesan cheese and serve.

Note: With practice the sauce can be made in 20 minutes. The reserved juice from the tomatoes can be frozen and used in a casserole or soup at a later date.

Serves 6

ingredients

500g/1 lb linguine or thin spaghetti

Puttanesca sauce
2 tablespoons olive oil
5 cloves garlic, crushed
4 x 440g/14oz cans peeled Italian plum tomatoes, drained and chopped
6 anchovy fillets, coarsely chopped
60g/2oz stoned black olives
2 tablespoons capers, drained and chopped
1 teaspoon dried oregano
¼ teaspoon chilli powder
½ bunch flat-leaved parsley, coarsely chopped
30g/1oz grated Parmesan cheese

fettuccine
with mushrooms

Method:

1 Cook pasta in boiling water in a large saucepan following packet directions. Drain, add 15g/1/2oz butter, toss, set aside and keep warm.

2 Heat oil and remaining butter in a frying pan over a medium heat, add mushrooms and cook, stirring, for 5 minutes or until the mushrooms start to give up their juices. Season to taste with black pepper. Sprinkle with parsley and cook for 1 minute longer.

3 Spoon mushrooms and pan juices over pasta, toss and sprinkle with Parmesan cheese.

Serves 4

ingredients

500g/1 lb fettuccine
30g/1oz butter
2 tablespoons olive oil
315g/10oz mushrooms, thinly sliced
freshly ground black pepper
3 tablespoons chopped flat-leaved parsley
4 tablespoons grated Parmesan cheese

creamy
mushroom gnocchi

Method:

1 Place potatoes in a bowl and mash. Add flour, butter, half the Parmesan cheese and black pepper to taste and mix to make a stiff dough. Turn dough onto a lightly floured surface and knead until smooth. Shape dough into 2¹/₂cm/1in ovals and press with the back of a fork.

2 Cook gnocchi, in batches, in boiling water in a large saucepan for 3 minutes or until they rise to the surface. Using a slotted spoon, remove gnocchi from pan and place in a greased shallow, ovenproof dish.

3 To make sauce, melt butter in a frying pan over a medium heat, add mushrooms and cook, stirring, for 5 minutes. Stir in mustard and cream and bring to the boil, reduce heat and simmer for 10 minutes or until sauce reduces and thickens.

4 Spoon sauce over gnocchi. Sprinkle with tasty cheese (mature cheddar) and Parmesan cheese and bake for 10-15 minutes or until cheese melts.

Note: For a delicious alternative, shred 250g/8oz English spinach and blanch in boiling water for 1 minute. Drain well and squeeze to remove as much liquid as possible, then stir into potato mixture. Serve gnocchi with crusty bread and a salad of crisp vegetables and mixed lettuces.

Serves 4

ingredients

500g/1 lb potatoes, cooked
2 cups/250g/8oz flour, sifted
30g/1oz butter, melted
30g/1oz grated Parmesan cheese
freshly ground black pepper

Mushroom sauce
30g/1oz butter
125g/4oz button mushrooms, sliced
2 tablespoons wholegrain mustard
1 cup/250mL/8fl oz cream (double)
60g/2oz grated tasty cheese
(mature cheddar)
30g/1oz grated Parmesan cheese

Oven temperature 180°C, 350°F, Gas 4

23

spaghetti
with tuna and olives

Method:

1 Cook spaghetti in boiling water in a large saucepan following packet directions. Drain and set aside to keep warm.

2 To make sauce, heat reserved oil from tuna in a frypan and cook onion, pepper and garlic for 3-4 minutes or until onion is soft. Stir in tomato puree, tomato paste and wine and cook for 3-4 minutes.

3 Add tuna to sauce and cook, stirring gently, for 4-5 minutes. Spoon sauce over spaghetti and toss to combine. Garnish with black pepper, parsley and olives.

Serves 4

ingredients

500g tubular spaghetti

Tuna sauce
440g canned tuna in oil, drained & oil reserved
1 large onion, chopped
1 green pepper, sliced
1 teaspoon minced garlic
1 1/2 cups/375g tomato puree
1 tablespoon tomato paste
1/2 cup/125mL white wine
1 tablespoon cracked black pepper
2 tablespoons finely chopped fresh parsley
8 pitted black olives, halved

fettuccine
bacon and cream

Method:

1 Cook fettuccine in boiling water in a large saucepan following packet directions. Drain and set aside to keep warm.

2 To make sauce, cook bacon in a large frypan for 4-5 minutes or until crisp. Add shallots, and cook for 1 minute longer. Stir in cream and stock, bring to the boil then reduce heat and simmer until reduced and thickened. Stir in sun-dried tomatoes and toss fettuccine in cream sauce. Sprinkle with Parmesan cheese and serve.

Serving suggestion: *A crisp salad and crusty bread is all that is needed to finish this course.*

Serves 4

ingredients

500g/1lb dried fettuccine
4 tablespoons grated Parmesan cheese

<u>Bacon and cream sauce</u>
2 rashers of bacon, trimmed and chopped
4 green shallots, chopped
¹/₂ cup/125 mL cream
¹/₂ cup/125mL chicken stock
3 tablespoons chopped sun-dried tomatoes (optional)

kingfish potato casserole

simple
seafood

Fish is one of the healthiest main meal

foods that you can eat and one of the quickest to cook.
The recipes in this section range from simple Salmon
Croquettes to a terrific Tuna and Macaroni Bake.

speedy
bouillabaisse

ingredients

2 teaspoons olive oil
2 onions, chopped
2 cloves garlic, crushed
I fresh red chilli, chopped
250g/8oz uncooked medium prawns,
peeled and deveined
16 mussels, scrubbed and beards removed
16 scallops, cleaned
440g/14oz canned spicy tomato soup
2 cups/500mL/16fl oz fish or chicken stock
125g/4oz squid (calamari) rings
2 tablespoons chopped fresh mixed herbs

Method:

1 Heat oil in a large frying pan over a medium heat, add onions, garlic and chilli and cook, stirring, for 4 minutes or until onions are soft.
2 Add prawns and cook for I minute. Add mussels, scallops, soup and stock and bring to simmering.
3 Stir in squid (calamari) and herbs and cook for I minute longer or until seafood is cooked.
Serving suggestion: Serve with quick-cooking brown rice or pasta.
Serves 4

kingfish
potato casserole

Photograph page 27

ingredients

6 medium potatoes
30g/1oz butter
85mL/2¹/₂fl oz hot milk
300mL/10fl oz sour cream
I small onion (finely chopped)
6 kingfish fillets
65g/2oz dry breadcrumbs
2 tablespoons cheese (grated)
ground paprika

Method:

1 Preheat oven to moderate temperature 200°C/400°/Gas 6.
2 Boil potatoes. When cooked, mash with butter and hot milk. Spread potato into the bottom of a large, shallow, greased casserole dish.
3 Spread one third of the sour cream over the potatoes, and spoon chopped onion over.
4 Arrange fish on top. Sprinkle with combined breadcrumbs and cheese. Spread remaining sour cream over crumb mixture, and sprinkle with paprika.
5 Bake in the moderately hot preheated oven for 30 minutes.
Serves 6

Oven temperature 200°C, 400°F, Gas 6

salmon
croquettes

Method:

1 Combine potato, onion, salmon, mustard, mayonnaise and egg, season to taste. Shape mixture into croquettes and roll in cookie crumbs to coat.

2 Heat oil in a frypan. Cook croquettes over medium heat until golden brown. Drain on absorbent paper.

Serves 4

ingredients

**3 large potatoes,
cooked and mashed
1 onion, grated
440g/14oz canned pink salmon,
drained and flaked
1 teaspoon Dijon-style mustard
2 tablespoons mayonnaise
1 egg, beaten
220g/7oz cheese flavoured cookies,
crushed
polyunsaturated oil for cooking**

barbequed
shark and vegetables with orange vinaigrette

Photograph page 31

barbequed shark and vegetables with orange vinaigrette

ingredients

1kg/2lb fresh shark steaks (cut into chunks about 2¹/₂cm/1in-thick)
2 red or yellow capsicums (pierced once with a knife)
12 small red-skinned potatoes (washed)
orange vinaigrette (see below)
3 zucchini (ends trimmed)
1 head radicchio (red chicory)

Method:

1 *Cut the shark into 6 even pieces. Set aside.*
2 *Heat a barbecue (until coals are medium-hot). Pierce capsicums with a knife and place on the hottest part of the grill. The skin should blister and char slightly after 12 minutes. Place in an airtight plastic lock bag. Allow to steam and cool. When cool enough to handle, peel away the skin and discard it.*
3 *If desired, thread all the potatoes on metal skewers. Place them over the hottest part of the fire. Cook for 25-30 minutes (turning occasionally, and basting with the orange vinaigrette).*
4 *Add zucchini, and cook (until slightly blackened, but tender). Baste occasionally with orange vinaigrette. (Zucchini will require about 8-10 minutes total cooking time.)*
5 *Add the shark steaks, and cook (for 6 minutes per side). Baste occasionally with orange vinaigrette. Slice radicchio in half lengthwise, and add to grill. Baste with vinaigrette. Cook for 4-5 minutes, until leaves are wilted and slightly charred. Remove all vegetables and fish from grill. Keep warm.*

6 *Transfer remaining orange vinaigrette to a microwave-safe container. Cook on high (100%) power for 2 minutes, stirring occasionally (until mixture boils). Drizzle over hot vegetables and fish, and serve.*

Serves 6

ORANGE VINAIGRETTE

Ingredients
2 tablespoons olive oil
1 teaspoon chopped ginger
1 tablepoon soy sauce
1 teaspoon orange rind
250mL/8fl oz orange juice
2 tablespoons balsamic vinegar
pinch cayenne pepper
1 teaspoon dry mustard

Method
1 *Combine all ingredients. Blend well. Transfer to a container with an air-tight lid. Shake vigerously before serving.*
2 *Dressing can be made up to one week in advance*

tomato
basil trout

Method:

1 Heat oil in a large frying pan, add spring onions and garlic and cook for 1 minute. Add trout to pan, pour over wine and top with tomatoes, basil and black pepper to taste. Cover and simmer for 10 minutes or until fish flakes when test with a fork.

Serving suggestion: Vegetables and crispy potato wedges are the perfect accompaniment to this dish. To make potato wedges, cut small potatoes into wedges and boil or microwave until tender. Drain and pat dry. Toss potatoes with 1/4 teaspoon chilli powder, 1 teaspoon ground turmeric, 1/2 teaspoon garam masala, 1 teaspoon ground coriander and 1/2 teaspoon ground ginger to coat. Shallow-fry for 5-10 minutes or until potatoes are crisp.

Note: Trout freezes well and keeping a few trout in your freezer ensures that you always have a basis for a tasty meal.

Remember when freezing any fish or shellfish that it has a shorter freezer life than meat or chicken because of the higher proportion of polyunsaturated fats in it. Frozen fish is best used within 3 months of freezing and should be cooked directly from frozen, this ensures that it holds its shape and retains its flavour and texture.

Serves 4

ingredients

2 teaspoons vegetable oil
4 spring onions, chopped
1 clove garlic, crushed
4 small trout, cleaned
3/4 cup/185mL/6fl oz red wine
4 tomatoes, chopped
4 tablespoons chopped fresh basil
freshly ground black pepper

parmesan
crusted fish

Method:

1 Pat fish dry. Combine flour, paprika and black pepper to taste. Combine breadcrumbs and Parmesan cheese. Coat fillets with flour mixture. Dip in egg, then coat with breadcrumb mixture. Heat oil in a frying pan over a medium heat, add fillets and cook for 2-3 minutes each side or until cooked.

2 To make Lemon Thyme Butter, heat butter, lemon rind, lemon juice and thyme in a saucepan over a medium heat for 1 minute or until butter melts. Serve with fish fillets.

Serving suggestion: *Accompany with potato crisps and vegetables. To make crisps, using a vegetable peeler, peel thin slices from potatoes. Dry slices and deep-fry for 7-10 minutes or until cooked. Drain and sprinkle with salt.*

Serves 4

ingredients

4 firm white fish fillets
¹/₂ cup/60g/2oz flour
1 teaspoon paprika
freshly ground pepper
1 cup/125g/4oz dried breadcrumbs
90g/3oz grated Parmesan cheese
1 egg, lightly beaten
2 tablespoons olive oil

Lemon thyme butter
60g/2oz butter
1 tablespoon grated lemon rind
1 tablespoon lemon juice
1 tablespoon chopped fresh thyme
or lemon thyme

unbelievable
salmon quiche

Photograph page 35

ingredients

½ cup/60g/2oz flour
5 eggs
60g/2oz butter, softened
220g/7oz canned red salmon,
drained and flaked
1 onion, diced
freshly ground black pepper
60g/2oz grated tasty cheese
(mature cheddar)

Method:
1 *Place flour, eggs and butter in a food processor and process to combine.*
2 *Pour egg mixture into a pie plate. Top with salmon, onion and black pepper to taste, then sprinkle with cheese and bake for 35-40 minutes or until mixture is set and top is brown.*

Note: *As this quiche cooks a crust forms on the bottom of it.*

For variety, canned tuna, cooked bacon, ham or chopped cooked chicken or turkey can be used in place of the salmon to make this magic recipe.

Serves 4

Oven temperature 180°C, 350°F, Gas 4

---

tuna
and macaroni bake

Photograph page 35

ingredients

60g/2oz butter
2 tablespoons flour
1 teaspoon dry mustard
1½ cups/375mL/12fl oz milk
2 teaspoons lemon juice
220g/7oz canned tuna,
drained and flaked
90g/3oz elbow macaroni or other small
pasta, cooked
125g/4oz grated tasty cheese
(mature cheddar)
freshly ground black pepper

Method:
1 *Melt butter in a saucepan over a medium heat, stir in flour and cook for 1 minute. Remove pan from heat, add mustard and slowly stir in milk and lemon juice. Return pan to heat and cook, stirring constantly, for 5 minutes or until sauce boils and thickens.*
2 *Stir in tuna, pasta, half the cheese and black pepper to taste. Spoon mixture into a greased shallow ovenproof dish, sprinkle with remaining cheese and bake for 20 minutes or until cheese melts and top is golden.*

Note: *A great way to use up leftover pasta, this traditional family favourite is also delicious made with canned salmon, ham leftover cooked chicken or turkey in place of the tuna.*

Serves 4

Oven temperature 180°C, 350°F, Gas 4

chicken tacos

family
favourites

It's great to come home to the

mouthwatering aroma of a home made pizza. This chapter
also includes vegetarian dishes and tasty grilled chicken that is
bound to become a family favourite.

ginger
beef with cashews

Method:

1 Using a sharp knife, slice meat thinly across the grain.
2 Heat oil in a wok or frying pan over a medium heat, add garlic and ginger and stir-fry for 1 minute. Increase heat to high, add beef and stir-fry for 2-3 minutes or until meat is brown.
3 Add cabbage, red pepper, bean sprouts and soy sauce and stir-fry for 2 minutes or until cabbage just starts to wilt.
4 Divide noodles between serving plates, top with beef mixture and scatter with cashews.
Serves 4

ingredients

500g/1 lb lean sirloin or rump steak
1 tablespoon vegetable oil
2 cloves garlic, crushed
1 teaspoon finely grated fresh ginger
¹/₂ Chinese cabbage (pak choi), shredded
¹/₂ red pepper (capsicum), sliced thinly
30g/1oz bean sprouts
1¹/₂ tablespoons soy sauce
3 x 75g/2¹/₂oz packets quick-cooking noodles, cooked and kept warm
60g/2oz raw cashews, roasted

chicken tacos

Photograph page 37

Method:

1 To make filling, heat oil in a frying pan, add onion, spring onions and tomatoes and cook, stirring, for 4 minutes. Add chicken, taco seasoning mix and salsa and cook, stirring, for 2 minutes longer or until heated through.
2 Spoon filling into taco shells and top with lettuce, red pepper, cheese, avocado and sour cream.

Serving suggestion: Accompany with a celery salad and crusty bread. To make salad, combine 2 tablespoons olive oil, 2 tablespoons white wine vinegar, 1 teaspoon Dijon mustard and freshly ground black pepper to taste, spoon over sliced celery and toss to combine.

Note: Remember to make turning the oven on the first step when you are preparing a meal that requires you to cook in it.
Serves 4

ingredients

12 taco shells, warmed
8 lettuce leaves, shredded
1 red pepper (capsicum), thinly sliced
125g/4oz tasty cheese (mature cheddar), grated
1 avocado, stoned, peeled and sliced
¹/₂ cup/125g/4oz sour cream

Chicken filling
2 teaspoons vegetable oil
1 onion, chopped
2 spring onions, chopped
3 tomatoes, chopped
1 kg/2 lb cooked chicken, skin removed and flesh shredded
2 tablespoons taco seasoning mix
4 tablespoons bottled tomato salsa

burgers
with a lot

Method:

1 *Place ground beef, breadcrumbs, egg and parsley in a bowl and mix to combine. Shape mixture into six patties.*
2 *Heat oil in a frying pan over a medium heat, add patties and cook for 3 minutes each side or until cooked to your liking.*
3 *Cut rolls in half and toast under a preheated medium grill for 2-3 minutes each side or until golden. Spread bottom halves of rolls with tomato relish and top each with a pattie, a lettuce leaf, some alfalfa sprouts, some beetroot, a slice of cheese and top half of roll.*

Serving suggestion: *Accompany with oven fries and coleslaw. To make coleslaw, place finely shredded cabbage, grated carrot, chopped celery, chopped red pepper (capsicum) and grated tasty cheese (mature cheddar) in a large bowl, add 3-4 tablespoons creamy or coleslaw dressing and toss to combine. Sprinkle with chopped fresh parsley.*

Note: *Many fresh salads are available from supermarkets and delicatessans. When time is really short these salads are a great timesaver.*

Serves 6

ingredients

500g/1 lb lean ground beef
³/₄ cup/45g/1¹/₂oz wholemeal breadcrumbs, made from stale bread
1 egg, lightly beaten
1 tablespoon chopped fresh parsley
1 tablespoon vegetable oil
6 wholegrain rolls
4 tablespoons tomato relish
6 lettuce leaves
60g/2oz alfalfa sprouts
1 raw beetroot, peeled and grated
6 slices Swiss cheese such as Emmental

fish
and chips

ingredients

500g/1 lb oven fries
vegetable oil for shallow-frying
4 boneless firm white fish fillets

Beer batter
1 cup/125g/4oz flour
2 egg whites
³/₄ cup/185mL/6fl oz beer
1 tablespoon vegetable oil

Method:
1 To make batter, place flour in a bowl and make a well in the centre. Add egg whites, beer and 1 tablespoon vegetable oil and mix until smooth.
2 Cook oven fries according to packet directions.
3 Heat 5cm/2in oil in a frying pan over a medium heat until a cube of bread dropped in browns in 50 seconds. Dip fish into batter, add to pan and cook for 3 minutes each side or until golden brown. Drain on absorbent kitchen paper. Serve with oven fries.
Serving suggestion: Accompany with a salad or vegetables of your choice.
Note: Get to know your supermarket and write shopping lists according to the layout of the shelves.
Serves 4

super
steak sandwiches

Method:

1 Heat oil in a frying pan over a high heat, add onions and cook, stirring, for 2-3 minutes or until onions are soft. Push onions to side of pan, add steaks and pineapple rings and cook for 2 minutes each side or until steak is cooked to your liking.

2 Top 4 slices of toast each with a slice of cheese, 2 slices tomato, a lettuce leaf, a steak, some onions, a pineapple ring, a spoonful of tomato or barbecue sauce and remaining toast slices. Serve immediately.

Serving suggestion: Serve with oven fries or potatoes and coleslaw.

Note: Steak sandwiches can also be cooked on the barbecue; rather than cooking in a frying pan cook on a lightly oiled preheated medium barbecue plate (griddle).

Serves 4

ingredients

2 teaspoons vegetable oil
2 onions, chopped
4 small lean rump steaks
4 canned pineapple rings, drained
8 thick slices wholemeal bread, toasted
4 slices tasty cheese (mature cheddar)
8 slices tomato
4 lettuce leaves
tomato or barbecue sauce

mixed
vegetable omelette

Method:

1 Melt 60g/2oz butter in a frypan, add leek, vegetables, garlic and mustard seed. Stir over medium heat for 5 minutes or until vegetables are just tender, remove from pan and keep warm.

2 Beat eggs and water together until fluffy, season to taste. Melt remaining butter in pan. Pour in half the egg mixture and cook until set. Spoon half the vegetable mixture onto omelette and fold over. Repeat with remaining egg mixture and vegetables.

Timesaver: Using some of the frozen mixed vegetable varieties for this recipe cuts down on preparation time as the chopping of the vegetables is eliminated. The cooking will remain the same.

Serves 2

ingredients

90g/3oz butter
1 leek, washed and sliced
1 1/2 cups/375g finely chopped mixed vegetables of your choice
1 clove garlic, crushed
1 teaspoon mustard seed
6 eggs
3 tablespoons water

vegetarian
pie

Method:

1 Combine rice, cheeses, shallots, zucchini, carrot, asparagus, pine nuts, eggs and yoghurt. Season with pepper.

2 Spoon mixture into a deep well-greased 23cm/9in springform pan. Bake at 190°C/370°C/Gas 5 for 40 minutes or until firm. Cut into wedges to serve.

Serves 6

ingredients

2 cups/300g cooked brown rice
1²/₃ cups/225g grated tasty cheese
4 tablespoons grated Parmesan cheese
2 shallots, chopped
2 zucchini, grated
1 carrot, peeled and grated
1 cup/150g canned asparagus cuts, drained
3 tablespoons pine nuts, toasted
3 eggs, lightly beaten
220g/7oz unflavoured yoghurt
freshly ground black pepper

Oven temperature 190°C, 370°F, Gas 5

43

fast
lamb curry

Method:

1 Heat oil in a wok or frying pan over a medium heat, add curry paste and cumin and cook, stirring, for 1 minute. Add lamb and stir-fry for 3 minutes or until lamb changes colour and is tender. Remove lamb mixture from pan and set aside.

2 Add red pepper (capsicum), zucchini (courgettes), broccoli and cauliflower to pan and stir-fry for 2 minutes. Stir in coconut milk and stock, bring to simmering and simmer for 4 minutes. Return lamb to pan and cook for 2 minutes longer or until heated through.

Serving suggestion: Serve with rice or noodles and poppadums.

Serves 4

ingredients

2 teaspoons vegetable oil
1 tablespoon curry paste
1 teaspoon ground cumin
500g/1 lb lean lamb fillets, cut into strips
1 red pepper (capsicum), cut into strips
2 zucchini (courgettes), sliced
250g/8oz broccoli florets
250g/8oz cauliflower,
broken into small florets
1 cup/250mL/8fl oz coconut milk
1/2 cup/125mL/4fl oz beef stock

grilled
chicken in pesto

Method:

1 Heat oil in a char-grill or frying pan over a high heat. Add chicken and cook for 4-5 minutes each side or until cooked through. Set aside and keep warm.

2 Add red pepper (capsicum), green peppe (capsicum)r, zucchini (courgettes) and eggplant (aubergines) to pan and cook for 2 minutes each side or until soft.

3 To make sauce, place pesto, mayonnaise, vinegar and black pepper to taste in bowl and mix to combine. To serve, arrange vegetables on serving plates, top with chicken and a spoonful of sauce.

Serving suggestion: Accompany with crusty bread.

Note: This recipe is ideal for cooking on the barbecue. Instead of cooking the chicken and vegetables in a char-grill or frying pan, simply cook on a lightly oiled preheated medium barbecue grill.

ingredients

2 teaspoons vegetable oil
4 boneless chicken breast fillets
I red pepper (capsicum), quartered
I green pepper (capsicum), quartered
2 zucchini (courgettes), halved lengthwise
2 baby eggplant (aubergines),
halved lengthwise

Pesto sauce
¹/₂ cup/125g/4oz ready-made pesto
¹/₂ cup/125g/4oz mayonnaise
2 tablespoons balsamic or red
wine vinegar
freshly ground black pepper

chicken
parcels

Method:

1 Melt butter in a frying pan, add mushrooms and spring onions and cook for 3 minutes. Remove pan from heat, add chicken, sour cream and black pepper to taste and set aside.

2 Roll out pastry to 5mm/¹/₄in thick and cut out four 18cm/7in rounds. Divide chicken mixture into four portions and place one portion on one half of each pastry round. Fold over other half of pastry and press edges to seal. Place parcels on a baking tray, brush with egg and bake for 15 minutes or until pastry is golden.

Serving suggestion: Delicious served with a salad of spinach and grilled bacon. To make salad, tear spinach leaves into pieces and place in a bowl. Scatter with grilled bacon pieces and chopped sun-dried tomatoes. Combine 2 tablespoons olive oil, 2 tablespoons balsamic or red wine vinegar and freshly ground black pepper to taste, spoon over salad and toss.

Serves 4

ingredients

15g/¹/₂oz butter
375g/12oz button mushrooms, halved
3 spring onions, chopped
1 kg/2 lb cooked chicken, skin removed and flesh chopped
³/₄ cup/185g/6oz sour cream
freshly ground black pepper
500g/1 lb prepared shortcrust pastry
1 egg, lightly beaten

mustard
crusted steaks

Method:

1 To make crust, place mustard, garlic, honey and mayonnaise in a small bowl and mix to combine. Spread mustard mixture over steaks.

2 Heat oil in a frying pan over a high heat, add steaks and cook for 2 minutes each side or until cooked to your liking.

Serving suggestion: An unusual accompaniment is broccoli with browned garlic. To make, divide a large head of broccoli into small florets, then boil, steam or microwave it until just tender. Refresh under cold running water. Divide a head of garlic into individual cloves and peel each clove. Heat 3 tablespoons olive oil in a frying pan, add garlic and cook, stirring, for 5-7 minutes or until garlic is brown. Take care that the garlic does not burn. Add broccoli to pan and cook, stirring, for 2-3 minutes or until heated. To complete the meal add mashed potatoes and finish with Caramel Chip Ice Cream.

Serves 4

ingredients

4 lean beef fillet steaks
2 teaspoons vegetable oil

<u>Mustard crust</u>
4 tablespoons wholegrain mustard
1 clove garlic, crushed
1 tablespoon honey
2 tablespoons mayonnaise

Oven temperature 230°C, 450°F, Gas 8

pizzas

Method:

1 *To assemble pizzas, spread bases with pasta sauce or tomato paste (purée).*
2 *For Supreme pizza, top a prepared pizza base with ham, salami, green peppe (capsicum)r, pineapple pieces, mushrooms and olives, if using.*
3 *For Hawaiian pizza, top a prepared pizza base with ham, pineapple pieces and red pepper (capsicum).*
4 *For Vegetarian pizza, top a prepared pizza base with mushrooms, red pepper (capsicum), broccoli and onion.*
5 *Sprinkle pizzas with cheese, place on baking trays and bake for 20 minutes at 230°C/450°F/Gas 8 or until base is crisp and golden.*

Serving suggestions: *All that pizzas require to make a complete meal is a tossed green salad.*

Serves 4-6

ingredients

3 large purchased pizza bases
1¹/₂ cups/375mL/12fl oz pasta sauce or tomato paste (purée)
375g/12oz mozzarella cheese or tasty cheese (mature cheddar), grated

<u>Supreme topping</u>
8 slices ham, chopped
6 slices spicy salami
¹/₂ green pepper (capsicum), chopped
125g/4oz canned pineapple pieces, drained
125g/4oz button mushrooms, sliced
60g/2oz pitted olives (optional)

<u>Hawaiian topping</u>
10 slices ham, shredded
185g/6oz canned pineapple pieces, drained
¹/₂ red pepper (capsicum), chopped

<u>Vegetarian topping</u>
250 g/8 oz button mushrooms, sliced
1/2 red pepper (capsicum), chopped
155g/5oz broccoli, broken into small florets
1 small onion, sliced

red
wine steaks

Method:

1 *To make marinade, place garlic, red wine, sugar and black pepper to taste in a shallow glass or ceramic dish. Add steaks, turn to coat and marinate for 5 minutes. Turn over and marinate for 5 minutes longer. Drain steaks and reserve marinade.*

2 *Heat oil in a frying pan over a high heat, add steaks and cook for 1-2 minutes each side or until cooked to your liking. Remove steaks from pan, set aside and keep warm. Add reserved marinade to pan and boil until reduced by half. Spoon sauce over steaks and serve immediately.*

Serving suggestion: *Serve with peppered fettuccine and vegetables. For fettuccine, toss hot fettucine with 1 tablespoon olive oil and 1 tablespoon coarsely crushed black peppercorns.*

Serves 4

ingredients

**4 veal or pork steaks
2 teaspoons vegetable oil**

**<u>Red wine marinade</u>
2 cloves garlic, crushed
³/₄ cup/185mL/6fl oz red wine
3 tablespoons brown sugar
freshly ground black pepper**

49

chicken and penne salad

simple
salads

Salads are becoming increasingly

Salads are becoming increasingly popular as main courses. These substantial salads are one-dish meals. You might like to try a Tuna and bean salad, Italian potato salad or a Salad nicoise. Accompany with crusty French bread or wholemeal rolls for for a complete meal.

carrot
and sultana salad

Method:
1 Place carrots and sultanas in a serving bowl.
2 To make dressing, place orange juice and honey in a small bowl and whisk to combine. Spoon dressing over carrot mixture and toss to combine. Sprinkle with nuts, cover and refrigerate until required.
Serves 10

ingredients
6 carrots, grated
125g/4oz sultanas
60g/2oz chopped nuts

Orange dressing
¼ cup/60mL/2fl oz orange juice
2 tablespoons honey

chicken
and penne salad

Photograph page 51

Method:
1 Arrange penne, chicken, green pepper (capsicum), chives, sweet corn, celery, tomatoes and endive on a large serving platter or in a large salad bowl. Spoon dressing over salad and serve immediately.
Serving suggestion: This salad is delicious served with chilli toast cheese. To make toast cheese, trim crusts from slices of white or wholemeal bread and cook under a preheated medium grill for 2-3 minutes or until toasted on one side. Top untoasted side with grated cheese and a pinch of chilli powder and cook for 2-3 minutes longer or until cheese melts and is golden.
Serves 4

ingredients

500g/1 lb penne, cooked
**1 kg/2 lb cooked chicken, skin removed
and flesh shredded**
1 green pepper (capsicum), chopped
3 tablespoons snipped fresh chives
**440g/14oz canned sweet corn
kernels, drained**
2 stalks celery, chopped
**250g/8oz yellow teardrop or
red cherry tomatoes**
250g/8oz curly endive
¾ cup/185mL/6fl oz creamy salad dressing

warm
seafood salad

Method:

1 Arrange watercress and lettuce leaves on individual dinner plates.

2 In a non-stick frypan, heat oil and cook onion and garlic until soft. Add scallops, prawns (shrimp) and fish and cook for 5-6 minutes or until prawns turn pink and fish is just cooked. Season with pepper. Arrange fish mixture over lettuce leaves.

3 To make dressing, combine lime juice, oil, pepper and dill in a screwtop jar and shake well to combine. Sprinkle over fish, garnish with dill sprigs and serve immediately.

Note: Our warm seafood salad makes a marvellous light meal in spring or autumn when there is a slight chill in the air.

Serves 6

ingredients

¹/₂ bunch watercress
mignonette lettuce leaves
butter lettuce leaves
1 tablespoon olive oil
1 onion, thinly sliced
1 clove garlic, crushed
315g/10oz scallops, cleaned
220g/7oz prawns (shrimp), shelled and deveined
250g/8oz firm white fish fillets
freshly ground black pepper
fresh dill sprigs for garnish

Dressing
¹/₂ cup/125mL lime juice
1 tablespoon olive oil
freshly ground black pepper
1 tablespoon finely chopped fresh dill

nutty
rice salad

Method:

1 Cook rice in boiling water in a large saucepan following packet directions or see instructions at the beginning of this chapter. Drain well and set aside to cool.
2 Boil, steam or microwave asparagus until just tender. Drain and refresh under cold running water. Set aside to cool completely. Cut into 5cm/2in pieces.
3 Heat oil in a frying pan over a medium heat. Add onions and cook, stirring occasionally, for 10 minutes or until onions are soft and golden. Set aside to cool.
4 Place rice, asparagus, onions, spring onions, tomatoes, pecans and sultanas in a salad bowl and toss to combine.
5 To make dressing, place garlic, mustard, orange juice and oil in a bowl and whisk to combine. Pour dressing over salad and toss to combine.

Serves 6

ingredients

2 cups/440g/7oz brown rice
250g/8oz asparagus spears, trimmed
1 tablespoon olive oil
3 onions, peeled and sliced
3 spring onions, sliced
3 tomatoes, chopped
60g/2oz chopped pecans
3 tablespoons sultanas

Orange dressing
1 clove garlic, peeled and crushed
1 teaspoon Dijon mustard
1/4 cup/60mL/2fl oz orange juice
1 tablespoon olive oil

potato
salad

Method:

1 Place potatoes in a saucepan, cover with cold water and bring to the boil. Reduce heat and simmer for 10-15 minutes or until potatoes are tender. Drain and set aside to cool.

2 Place eggs in a saucepan, cover with cold water and bring to the boil over a medium heat, then simmer for 10 minutes. Drain and cool under cold running water. Cool completely. Remove shells and cut into quarters.

3 Place bacon in a nonstick frying pan and cook over a medium heat, stirring occasionally, for 10 minutes or until crisp. Drain on absorbent kitchen paper.

4 Place potatoes, eggs, bacon, onion, spring onions, dill and mint in a salad bowl and toss gently to combine.

5 To make dressing, combine mayonnaise, yoghurt, mustard and black pepper to taste in a bowl. Spoon dressing over salad and toss to combine.

Serves 6

ingredients

1 kg/2 lb potatoes, peeled and cut into cubes
3 eggs
4 rashers bacon, rind removed, chopped
1 onion, peeled and finely chopped
2 spring onions, chopped
2 tablespoons chopped fresh dill
1 tablespoon chopped fresh mint

Mustard dressing
1 cup/250mL/8fl oz mayonnaise
3 tablespoons natural yoghurt
1 tablespoon Dijon mustard
freshly ground black pepper

italian
green bean salad

Photograph page 57

ingredients

**500g/1lb green beans, topped and tailed
6 shallots, finely chopped
3 tomatoes, peeled and chopped
8 black olives, stoned
freshly ground black pepper**

Dressing
**1 tablespoon olive oil
3 tablespoons lemon juice
1 clove garlic, crushed
1 tablespoon chopped fresh parsley
1 tablespoon finely chopped fresh chives
1 teaspoon finely chopped fresh rosemary
1 teaspoon finely chopped fresh thyme**

Method:
1 *Boil, steam or microwave beans until just tender. Refresh under cold running water.*
2 *Place beans, shallots, tomatoes and olives in a salad bowl.*
3 *To make dressing, place oil, lemon juice, garlic, parsley, chives, rosemary and thyme in a screwtop jar. Shake well to combine and pour over salad. Season with pepper and toss.*
Serves 4

tomato
and basil salad

Photograph page 57

ingredients

**750g/1¹/₂lb ripe tomatoes, peeled, sliced
4 tablespoons finely chopped fresh basil
2 tablespoons grated Parmesan cheese
freshly ground black pepper**

Dressing
**1 clove garlic, crushed
1 tablespoon olive oil
3 tablespoons white wine vinegar**

Method:
1 *Arrange tomato slices overlapping on a serving platter and sprinkle with basil leaves.*
2 *To make dressing, place garlic, oil and vinegar in a screwtop jar. Shake well to combine and sprinkle over tomatoes. Just before serving, sprinkle tomato salad with Parmesan cheese. Season with pepper.*
Note: *You might like to try a combination of cherry tomatoes and little yellow teardrop tomatoes to make this aromatic tomato salad look even more attractive.*
Serves 6

sweet
potato chip salad

Method:

1 *Preheat barbecue to a high heat. Brush sweet potato slices with oil. Cook sweet potatoes, in batches, on barbecue plate (griddle) for 4 minutes each side or until golden and crisp. Drain on absorbent kitchen paper.*

2 *Place spinach and rocket leaves, tomatoes, onions, olives and parmesan cheese shavings in a bowl and toss to combine. Cover and chill until required.*

3 *To make dressing, place oregano leaves, sugar, vinegar and black pepper to taste in a screwtop jar and shake to combine.*

4 *To serve, add sweet potato chips to salad, drizzle with dressing and toss to combine.*

Serves 8

ingredients

1 kg/2 lb sweet potatoes, thinly sliced
3-4 tablespoons olive oil
185g/6oz baby English spinach leaves
185g/6oz rocket leaves
3 tomatoes, chopped
2 red onions, sliced
4 tablespoons pitted black olives
60g/2oz parmesan cheese shavings

Sweet oregano dressing
2 tablespoons fresh oregano leaves
1 ¹/₂ tablespoons brown sugar
¹/₃ cup/90mL/3fl oz balsamic vinegar
freshly ground black pepper

marinated
zucchini salad

Method:

1 *Place zucchini (courgettes) and onion in a bowl.*
2 *To make dressing, place dill, parsley, garlic, vinegar, oil, lemon juice and black pepper to taste in bowl and whisk to combine. Pour over zucchini (courgette) mixture and toss. Cover and chill for at least 1 hour before serving.*

Serves 8

ingredients

6 zucchini (courgettes), sliced
1 onion, sliced

<u>Fresh herb dressing</u>
2 tablespoons chopped fresh dill
1 tablespoon chopped fresh parsley
1 clove garlic, crushed
¹/₄ cup/60mL/2fl oz white vinegar
2 tablespoons olive oil
1 tablespoon lemon juice
freshly ground black pepper

cauliflour parmesan

on the side

A sensational side dish can add

colour, flavour and variety to an otherwise simple meal. Many of these side dishes can also double as light meals. Delight the family by serving one of following dishes in this chapter, it's sure to be a success.

rosemary
potatoes

Method:

1 Bring a large saucepan of water to boil. Add potatoes. When water boils again, remove pan from heat and drain potatoes in a colander. Pat dry with paper towels.

2 Melt butter in a large frying pan over moderate heat. Add garlic, potato slices and rosemary.

3 Sauté potatoes until lightly golden and cooked through. Shake pan frequently to prevent them from sticking, and turn them over occasionally with a spatula. Serve at once, in a heated dish.

Serves 4

ingredients

500g/1lb potatoes, peeled and thinly sliced
60g/2oz butter
1 clove garlic, crushed
1 tablespoon finely chopped fresh rosemary

cauliflour
parmesan

Photograph page 61

Method:

1 Boil, steam or microwave cauliflower until just tender. Drain well and place in a lightly buttered shallow baking dish.

2 Melt butter in a saucepan over a medium heat, add breadcrumbs and cook, stirring, for 4-5 minutes or until golden. Remove pan from heat, add Parmesan cheese and black pepper to taste and mix to combine.

3 Sprinkle breadcrumb mixture over cauliflower and cook under a preheated hot grill for 3-5 minutes or until top is golden. Sprinkle with parsley and serve.

Note: For something different make this easy side dish using broccoli in place of the cauliflower or use a combination of broccoli and cauliflower.

Serves 6

ingredients

1 small cauliflower, broken into florets
60g/2oz butter
¾ cup/90g/3oz dried breadcrumbs
60 g/2 oz grated Parmesan cheese
freshly ground black pepper
2 tablespoons chopped flat-leaved parsley

braised
artichokes and beans

Method:

1 Melt butter in a frying pan over a medium heat, add garlic and onions and cook, stirring, for 3 minutes or until onions are soft.

2 Add carrots, beans, artichokes and stock and bring to the boil. Reduce heat and simmer for 10 minutes or until vegetables are tender. Season to taste with black pepper.

Serves 6

ingredients

30g/1oz butter
2 cloves garlic, crushed
2 onions, sliced
2 carrots, sliced
250g/8oz fresh broad beans, shelled or
125g/4oz frozen broad beans
440g/14oz canned artichoke hearts, drained
1 cup/250mL/8fl oz vegetable stock
freshly ground black pepper

beans
with cumin vinaigrette

Photograph page 65

Method:

1 *Boil, steam or microwave beans until just tender. Drain, refresh under cold running water and drain again.*
2 *Place beans and tomatoes in a salad bowl.*
3 *To make vinaigrette, place spring onions, mustard, cumin, oil, vinegar and black pepper to taste in a screwtop jar and shake well. Spoon dressing over bean mixture and toss to combine.*

Note: *Do not refrigerate this dish after making - the flavours will develop if it is left to stand at room temperature for a while.*

Serves 4

ingredients

500g/1 lb green beans, halved
12 cherry tomatoes, cut in half

Cumin vinaigrette
2 spring onions, finely chopped
1 teaspoon dry mustard
¹/₂ teaspoon ground cumin
¹/₂ cup/125mL/4fl oz olive oil
2 tablespoons wine vinegar
freshly ground black pepper

ratatouille

Photograph page 65

Method:

1 *Heat oil in a large saucepan over a medium heat, add onions and cook, stirring, for 5 minutes or until onions are lightly browned. Add green peppers (capsicums), and garlic and cook, stirring occasionally, for 5 minutes longer.*
2 *Add zucchini (courgettes), eggplant (aubergines), tomatoes, oregano, basil and marjoram and bring to the boil. Reduce heat and simmer, stirring occasionally, for 30 minutes or until mixture reduces and thickens and vegetables are well cooked. Season to taste with black pepper. Serve hot, warm or at room temperature.*

Note: *Red peppers, mushrooms and fresh herbs are all tasty additions to this popular side dish. With the addition of canned beans this becomes a great main meal for vegetarians. Drain and rinse the beans and add to the vegetable mixture in the last 5 minutes of cooking.*

Serves 6

ingredients

¹/₄ cup/60mL/2fl oz vegetable oil
2 onions, chopped
2 green peppers (capsicums), diced
2 cloves garlic, crushed
4 zucchini (courgettes), diced
2 eggplant (aubergines), diced
2 x 440g/14oz canned tomatoes, undrained and mashed
1 teaspoon dried oregano
1 teaspoon dried basil
1 teaspoon dried marjoram
freshly ground black pepper

potato
gratin

Method:

1 Layer potatoes, onions, chives and black pepper to taste in six lightly greased individual ovenproof dishes.
2 Place yogurt and cream in a bowl and mix to combine. Carefully pour yogurt mixture over potatoes and sprinkle with Parmesan cheese. Bake for 45 minutes or until potatoes are tender and top is golden.

Serves 6

ingredients

I kg/2 lb potatoes, thinly sliced
2 large onions, thinly sliced
2 tablespoons snipped fresh chives
freshly ground black pepper
I¹/₄ cup/250g/8oz low-fat natural yogurt
I cup/250mL/8fl oz cream (double)
60g/2oz grated Parmesan cheese

asparagus
in prosciutto

Method:

1 Preheat barbecue to a high heat.
2 Top each prosciutto slice with a basil leaf and an asparagus spear. Wrap prosciutto around asparagus to enclose.
3 Brush asparagus parcels with lemon juice and sprinkle with black pepper to taste. Place asparagus parcels on oiled barbecue and cook, turning frequently, until prosciutto is crisp and asparagus is tender.
4 To make dipping sauce, place mayonnaise, lemon juice and chopped basil in a bowl and mix to combine. Serve with asparagus parcels.

Serves 12

ingredients

**250g/8oz prosciutto slices
fresh basil leaves
500g/1 lb fresh asparagus spears
¹/₃ cup/90mL/3fl oz lemon juice
freshly ground black pepper**

Basil dipping sauce
**³/₄ cup/185mL/6fl oz whole
egg mayonnaise
2 tablespoons lemon juice
2 tablespoons chopped fresh basil**

dijon
mushrooms

Method:

1 Melt butter in a nonstick frying pan over a medium heat, add onions or shallots and garlic and cook, stirring, for 2-3 minutes or until onions or shallots are soft.

2 Add mushrooms and cook, stirring occasionally, for 5 minutes or until mushrooms are cooked. Remove mushrooms from pan, set aside and keep warm.

3 Stir wine, mustard and coriander into pan and bring to the boil. Reduce heat and simmer for 10 minutes or until liquid reduces by half. Remove pan from heat, stir in yoghurt and season to taste with black pepper. Return pan to a low heat, and cook for 2-3 minutes or until heated through. Spoon sauce over mushrooms, sprinkle with parsley and serve.

ingredients

30g/1oz butter
4 pickling onions or shallots, finely chopped
1 clove garlic, crushed
500g/1 lb mushrooms
³/₄ cup/185mL/6fl oz dry white wine
1 tablespoon Dijon mustard
1 teaspoon finely chopped fresh coriander
1¹/₄ cup/250g/8oz low-fat natural yoghurt
freshly ground black pepper
2 tablespoons chopped fresh parsley

Serves 4

barbecued
potato skins

Method:

1 Bake potatoes in the oven for 1 hour or until tender. Remove from oven and set aside until cool enough to handle. Cut potatoes in half and scoop out flesh leaving a 5mm/¹/₄in thick shell. Reserve potato flesh for another use. Cut potato skins into large pieces and brush with oil.

2 Preheat barbecue to a medium heat. Cook potato skins on lightly oiled barbecue grill for 5-8 minutes each side or until crisp and golden.

Serving suggestion: Potato skins are delicious served with a dip of your choice.

Cook's tip: The reserved potato flesh can be used to make a potato salad to serve at your barbecue. It could also be used to make a potato curry, as a topping on a cottage pie, or to make croquettes.

Serves 4

ingredients

6 large potatoes, scrubbed
olive oil

Oven temperature 200°C, 400°F, Gas 6

sticky date pudding

short
& sweet

A little something sweet and satisfying

for dessert is a favourite with everyone, but it needn't
take all day to prepare. Simply scrumptious sweets like
the recipes featured in this chapter can be assembled
using canned or fresh fruit, and look as though you've
spent hours in the kitchen.

apple
and apricot crumble

Method:

1 Place apricots, apples, sugar and cinnamon in a bowl and mix to combine. Spoon fruit mixture into a greased ovenproof dish.

2 To make topping, place rolled oats or muesli, coconut, butter and honey in bowl and mix to combine. Sprinkle topping over fruit mixture and bake for 30 minutes or until fruit is hot and topping is crisp and golden.

Note: Any canned fruit is delicious used in this dessert. For something different you might like to try plums and apples or pears and peaches.

Serves 6

ingredients

2 x 440g/14oz canned apricot halves, drained
440g/14oz canned sliced apples, drained
2 tablespoons brown sugar
¼ teaspoon ground cinnamon

Crumble topping
2 cups/185g/6oz rolled oats or muesli
30g/1oz shredded coconut
125g/4oz butter, melted
2 tablespoons honey

Oven temperature 180°C, 350°F, Gas 4

sticky
date pudding

Photograph page 71

Method:

1 Place dates and water in a saucepan and bring to the boil over a medium heat. Reduce heat and simmer for 5 minutes or until dates are soft. Remove pan from heat and stir in bicarbonate of soda. Set aside.

2 Place butter and sugar in a bowl and beat until light and creamy. Beat in eggs, one at a time, beating well after each addition. Fold in flour. Add date mixture and mix to combine.

3 Pour mixture into a lightly greased 18x28cm/7x11in cake tin and bake for 25 minutes or until cooked when tested with a skewer.

4 To make sauce, place butter and sugar in a saucepan and cook over a low heat, stirring constantly, for 4-5 minutes or until butter melts and ingredients are combined. Stir in cream, bring to simmering and simmer, stirring constantly, for 5 minutes or until sauce thickens. Pour sauce over hot pudding and serve immediately.

Serves 8

ingredients

155g/5oz pitted dates, chopped
2 cups/500mL/16fl oz water
1 teaspoon bicarbonate of soda
60g/2oz butter, softened
1¼ cups/220g/7oz brown sugar
2 eggs, lightly beaten
¾ cup/90g/3oz self-raising flour, sifted

Toffee cream sauce
60g/2oz butter
½ cup/90g/3oz brown sugar
¾ cup/185mL/6fl oz cream (double)

Oven temperature 180°C, 350°F, Gas 4

easy
chocolate cake

Method:

1. Place milk, butter and eggs in a bowl and whisk to combine.
2. Sift together flour and cocoa powder into a separate bowl. Add sugar and mix to combine. Make a well in the centre of the dry ingredients and pour in milk mixture. Beat for 5 minutes or until mixture is smooth.
3. Pour mixture into a greased 20cm/8in round cake tin and bake for 40 minutes or until cooked when tested with a skewer. Stand cake in tin for 5 minutes before turning onto a wire rack to cool.
4. To make icing, sift icing sugar and cocoa powder together into a bowl. Stir in milk and mix until smooth. Spread icing over cold cake.

Makes a 20cm/8in round cake

ingredients

1 cup/250mL/8fl oz milk
125g/4oz butter, softened
2 eggs, lightly beaten
1¹/₃ cups/170g/5¹/₂oz self-raising flour
²/₃ cup/60g/2oz cocoa powder
1 cup/220g/7oz caster sugar

<u>Chocolate icing</u>
1 cup/155g/5oz icing sugar
2 tablespoons cocoa powder
2 tablespoons milk

Oven temperature 180°C, 350°F, Gas 4

raspberry
mousse

Method:

1 Place raspberries in a food processor or blender and process to make a purée. Push purée through a sieve to remove seeds and set aside. Stir gelatine mixture into purée and set aside.

2 Place ricotta or curd cheese in a food processor or blender and process until smooth. Set aside.

3 Place egg yolks and sugar in a heatproof bowl, set over a saucepan of simmering water and beat until a ribbon trail forms when beater is lifted from mixture. Remove bowl from heat. Whisk egg yolk mixture, then ricotta or curd cheese into raspberry purée. Cover and chill until just beginning to set.

4 Place egg whites in a bowl and beat until stiff peaks form. Fold egg white mixture into fruit mixture. Spoon mousse mixture into four lightly oiled ¹/₂ cup/125mL/4fl oz capacity moulds or ramekins, cover and chill until set.

5 To serve, garnish with chocolate curls.

Serves 4

ingredients

**500g/1 lb fresh or frozen raspberries
2 teaspoons gelatine dissolved in
2 tablespoons hot water, cooled
125g/4oz ricotta or curd cheese, drained
4 eggs, separated
¹/₄ cup/60g/2oz caster sugar
whipped cream
chocolate curls, to garnish (optional)**

plum
clafoutis

Method:

1 Arrange plums, cut side down, in a lightly greased 25cm/10in flan dish.
2 Sift flour into a bowl and make a well in the centre. Break eggs into well, add caster sugar and milk and mix to form a smooth batter.
3 Pour batter over plums and bake for 45 minutes at 190°C/375°F or until firm and golden. Serve hot, warm or cold, sprinkled with icing sugar.

Serves 6

ingredients

500g/1 lb dark plums, halved and stoned, or 440g/14oz canned plums, well drained
1 cup/125g/4oz self-raising flour
3 eggs
¹/₂ cup/100g/3¹/₂oz caster sugar
¹/₂ cup/125mL/4fl oz reduced-fat milk
1 tablespoon icing sugar, sifted

Oven temperature 180°C, 350°F, Gas 4

new orleans
style bananas

Method:

1 Melt butter in a heavy-based saucepan over a medium heat, add sugar and cinnamon and cook, stirring, until sugar melts and mixture is combined.

2 Stir in liqueur or orange juice and half the rum and cook for 5 minutes or until mixture is thick and syrupy.

3 Add bananas and toss to coat with syrup. Add remaining rum, swirl pan and ignite immediately. Baste bananas with sauce until flame goes out.

4 To serve, divide bananas and ice cream between serving plates and drizzle sauce from pan over ice cream.

ingredients

60g/2oz unsalted butter
¼ cup/60g/2oz brown sugar
½ teaspoon ground cinnamon
¼ cup/60mL/2fl oz banana-flavoured liqueur or orange juice
½ cup/125mL/4fl oz dark rum
4 bananas, halved lengthwise
4 scoops vanilla ice cream

caramel
cherries

Method:

1 *Place cherries in a shallow ovenproof dish.*
2 *Place cream and liqueur or sherry in a bowl and beat until soft peaks form. Spoon cream mixture over cherries, sprinkle thickly with brown sugar and cook under a preheated hot grill for 3-4 minutes or until sugar melts. Serve immediately.*

Serves 6

ingredients

440g/14oz canned, pitted sweet cherries, drained
1¼ cups/315mL/10fl oz cream (double), whipped
1 teaspoon liqueur of your choice or sherry brown sugar

Cooking is not an exact science: one does not require finely calibrated scales, pipettes and scientific equipment to cook, yet the conversion to metric measures in some countries and its interpretations must have intimidated many a good cook.

Weights are given in the recipes only for ingredients such as meats, fish, poultry and some vegetables. Though a few grams/ounces one way or another will not affect the success of your dish.

Though recipes have been tested using the Australian Standard 250mL cup, 20mL tablespoon and 5mL teaspoon, they will work just as well with the US and Canadian 8fl oz cup, or the UK 300mL cup. We have used graduated cup measures in preference to tablespoon measures so that proportions are always the same. Where tablespoon measures have been given, these are not crucial measures, so using the smaller tablespoon of the US or UK will not affect the recipe's success. At least we all agree on the teaspoon size.

For breads, cakes and pastries, the only area which might cause concern is where eggs are used, as proportions will then vary. If working with a 250mL or 300mL cup, use large eggs (60g/2oz), adding a little more liquid to the recipe for 300mL cup measures if it seems necessary. Use the medium-sized eggs (55g/1$\frac{1}{4}$oz) with 8fl oz cup measure. A graduated set of measuring cups and spoons is recommended, the cups in particular for measuring dry ingredients. Remember to level such ingredients to ensure their accuracy.

English measures

All measurements are similar to Australian with two exceptions: the English cup measures 300mL/10fl oz, whereas the Australian cup measure 250mL/8fl oz. The English tablespoon (the Australian dessertspoon) measures 14.8mL/$\frac{1}{2}$fl oz against the Australian tablespoon of 20mL/$\frac{3}{4}$fl oz.

American measures

The American reputed pint is 16fl oz, a quart is equal to 32fl oz and the American gallon, 128fl oz. The Imperial measurement is 20fl oz to the pint, 40fl oz a quart and 160fl oz one gallon.

The American tablespoon is equal to 14.8mL/$\frac{1}{2}$fl oz, the teaspoon is 5mL/$\frac{1}{6}$fl oz. The cup measure is 250mL/8fl oz, the same as Australia.

Dry measures

All the measures are level, so when you have filled a cup or spoon, level it off with the edge of a knife. The scale below is the "cook's equivalent"; it is not an exact conversion of metric to imperial measurement. To calculate the exact metric equivalent yourself, use 2.2046 lb = 1kg or 1 lb = 0.45359kg

Metric		Imperial	
g = grams		oz = ounces	
kg = kilograms		lb = pound	
15g		$\frac{1}{2}$oz	
20g		$\frac{2}{3}$oz	
30g		1oz	
60g		2oz	
90g		3oz	
125g		4oz	$\frac{1}{4}$ lb
155g		5oz	
185g		6oz	
220g		7oz	
250g		8oz	$\frac{1}{2}$ lb
280g		9oz	
315g		10oz	
345g		11oz	
375g		12oz	$\frac{3}{4}$ lb
410g		13oz	
440g		14oz	
470g		15oz	
1,000g	1kg	35.2oz	2.2 lb
	1.5kg		3.3 lb

Oven temperatures

The Celsius temperatures given here are not exact; they have been rounded off and are given as a guide only. Follow the manufacturer's temperature guide, relating it to oven description given in the recipe. Remember gas ovens are hottest at the top, electric ovens at the bottom and convection-fan forced ovens are usually even throughout. We included Regulo numbers for gas cookers which may assist. To convert °C to °F multiply °C by 9 and divide by 5 then add 32.

Oven temperatures

	C°	F°	Regulo
Very slow	120	250	1
Slow	150	300	2
Moderately slow	150	325	3
Moderate	180	350	4
Moderately hot	190-200	370-400	5-6
Hot	210-220	410-440	6-7
Very hot	230	450	8
Super hot	250-290	475-500	9-10

Cake dish sizes

Metric	Imperial
15cm	6in
18cm	7in
20cm	8in
23cm	9in

Loaf dish sizes

Metric	Imperial
23x12cm	9x5in
25x8cm	10x3in
28x18cm	11x7in

Liquid measures

Metric	Imperial	Cup & Spoon
mL	fl oz	
millilitres	fluid ounce	
5mL	1/6fl oz	1 teaspoon
20mL	2/3fl oz	1 tablespoon
30mL	1fl oz	1 tablespoon plus 2 teaspoons
60mL	2fl oz	1/4 cup
85mL	2 1/2fl oz	1/3 cup
100mL	3fl oz	3/8 cup
125mL	4fl oz	1/2 cup
150mL	5fl oz	1/4 pint, 1 gill
250mL	8fl oz	1 cup
300mL	10fl oz	1/2 pint)
360mL	12fl oz	1 1/2 cups
420mL	14fl oz	1 3/4 cups
500mL	16fl oz	2 cups
600mL	20fl oz 1 pint,	2 1/2 cups
1 litre	35fl oz 1 3/4 pints,	4 cups

Cup measurements

One cup is equal to the following weights.

	Metric	Imperial
Almonds, flaked	90g	3oz
Almonds, slivered, ground	125g	4oz
Almonds, kernel	155g	5oz
Apples, dried, chopped	125g	4oz
Apricots, dried, chopped	190g	6oz
Breadcrumbs, packet	125g	4oz
Breadcrumbs, soft	60g	2oz
Cheese, grated	125g	4oz
Choc bits	155g	5oz
Coconut, desiccated	90g	3oz
Cornflakes	30g	1oz
Currants	155g	5oz
Flour	125g	4oz
Fruit, dried (mixed, sultanas etc)	185g	6oz
Ginger, crystallised, glace	250g	8oz
Honey, treacle, golden syrup	315g	10oz
Mixed peel	220g	7oz
Nuts, chopped	125g	4oz
Prunes, chopped	220g	7oz
Rice, cooked	155g	5oz
Rice, uncooked	220g	7oz
Rolled oats	90g	3oz
Sesame seeds	125g	4oz
Shortening (butter, margarine)	250g	8oz
Sugar, brown	155g	5oz
Sugar, granulated or caster	250g	8oz
Sugar, sifted icing	155g	5oz
Wheatgerm	60g	2oz

Length

Some of us still have trouble converting imperial length to metric. In this scale, measures have been rounded off to the easiest-to-use and most acceptable figures.

To obtain the exact metric equivalent in converting inches to centimetres, multiply inches by 2.54 whereby 1 inch equals 25.4 millimetres and 1 millimetre equals 0.03937 inches.

Metric	Imperial
mm=millimetres	in = inches
cm=centimetres	ft = feet
5mm, 0.5cm	1/4in
10mm, 1.0cm	1/2in
20mm, 2.0cm	3/4in
2.5cm	1in
5cm	2in
8cm	3in
10cm	4in
12cm	5in
15cm	6in
18cm	7in
20cm	8in
23cm	9in
25cm	10in
28cm	11in
30cm	1 ft, 12in

index